Chinese Culture

Mary Colson

Heinemann
LIBRARY
Chicago, Illinois

www.capstonepub.com
Visit our website to find out
more information about
Heinemann-Raintree books.

To order:
☎ Phone 800-747-4992
▣ Visit www.capstonepub.com
to browse our catalog and order online.

Edited by Charlotte Guillain, Abby Colich,
and Vaarunika Dharmapala
Designed by Steve Mead
Original illustrations © Capstone Global
Library Ltd 2013
Illustrations by Oxford Designers & Illustrators
Picture research by Ruth Blair

Originated by Capstone Global Library Ltd
Printed and bound in the United States of
America, North Mankato, Minnesota.

16 15 14 13
10 9 8 7 6 5 4 3 2

082013 007601RP

Library of Congress Cataloging-in-Publication
Data
Colson, Mary.
  Chinese culture / Mary Colson.—1st ed.
    p. cm.—(Global cultures)
  Includes bibliographical references and index.
  ISBN 978-1-4329-6777-2 (hb)—ISBN 978-
1-4329-6786-4 (pb) 1. Culture—History. 2.
China—Social life and customs. 3. China—
Civilization. I. Title.
  HM621.C64225 2013
  306.0951—dc23   2011037701

Acknowledgments
We would like to thank the following for
permission to reproduce photographs:
Alamy pp. 13 (© The Art Archive), 20 (©
Robert Harding Picture Library Ltd), 25 (©
John Warburton-Lee Photography), 29 (©
dbimages), 31 (© Jon Arnold Images Ltd),
37 (© Photos 12); Corbis pp. 5 (© Gong Lei/
Xinhua Press), 8 (© Royal Ontario Museum),
10 (© Justin Guariglia), 11 (© Peng Zhen Ge/
Redlink), 12 (© Fritz Hoffmann/In Pictures),
15 (© Gao Shanyue/Xinhua Press), 18 (©
Bettmann), 22 (© Jack Hollingsworth), 27
(© Blue Jean Images), 28 (© Christophe
Boisvieux), 36 (© Liu Liqun), 39 (© Steven
Vidler/Eurasia Press); Getty Images pp. 19
(Gamma-Keystone), 24 (RedChopsticks);
© Photoshot p. 41; Photoshot pp. 17 (©
Xinhua), 32 (© UPPA), 34, 35 (© Xinhua);
Shutterstock pp. 6 (© Roman Sigaev), 7 (©
Mikhail Nekrasov), 9 (© Stefano Tronci), 16
(© davidk), 23 (© Hung Chung Chih), 33 (©
Thomas Barrat), 43 top left (© Carlos Huang),
43 top right (© Hung Chung Chih), 43 bottom
left (© Ben Jeayes), 43 bottom right (© Jess
Yu), design features (© bluehand).

Cover photograph of a smiling Chinese
boy reproduced with permission of Alamy
(© Lonely Planet Images). Cover design feature
of a colorful textile reproduced with permission
of Shutterstock (© bluehand).

Every effort has been made to contact
copyright holders of any material reproduced
in this book. Any omissions will be rectified
in subsequent printings if notice is given to
the publisher.

CONTENTS

Some words are shown in bold, **like this**. You can find out what they mean by looking in the glossary.

INTRODUCING CHINESE CULTURE

What do you picture when you think of Chinese culture? Do you imagine dragons and temples? Or do you think of martial arts and chopsticks?

What is culture?

Culture includes the values, beliefs, and attitudes of a place. It is about how people live and worship, and about the music, art, and literature they produce. Chinese culture has developed over 4,000 years. This book explores different aspects of this ancient, colorful, and fascinating culture.

Powerful rulers

For thousands of years, different parts of China were ruled by powerful emperors from different families called **dynasties**. Some of the most important dynasties were:

Qin Dynasty	221–206 BCE
Han Dynasty	206 BCE –220 CE
Three Kingdoms	220–280 CE
Southern and Northern Dynasties	420–589 CE
Sui Dynasty	581–618 CE
Tang Dynasty	618–907 CE
Song Dynasty	960–1279 CE
Ming Dynasty	1368–1644 CE
Qing Dynasty	1644–1911/12 CE

Since 1912, China has been ruled by an elected government.

Lion dances are performed in China on special occasions such as New Year's Day.

Did you know?

There are over 1 billion people living in China. That is about one-seventh of the world's total population. Over 90 percent of people are Han Chinese, but there are many other **ethnic groups**, including Zhuang, Manchu, Yi, Miao, Uighur, Jinuo, and Dong.

ORNAMENT

Art and decoration are central to Chinese culture, from elaborate palaces and gardens to fine silk painting, paper cutting, and beautiful writing. Many of the grandest buildings and monuments in China were designed around ideas of power, **superstition**, and **harmony** in nature.

Feng shui is a way of creating harmony between buildings and nature to improve the quality of life. The Imperial Summer Palace (Qing Dynasty) and the Tiantan Temple (Ming Dynasty) were carefully built to follow the rules of *feng shui* by including ponds, wells, and even rivers.

Forbidden City

Beijing's Forbidden City was built during the Ming Dynasty, from 1406 to 1420. For over 500 years, the city was "forbidden" because ordinary people were not allowed to enter. Today, this huge complex of over 900 buildings and gardens is one of China's most important tourist attractions.

Today, the Forbidden City is popular with tourists.

Did you know?

Chinese people believe that evil things travel in straight lines, so roofs are often curved to prevent evil from entering buildings. Little statues called door gods are hung on doorways to ward off evil.

Changcheng: **The Great Wall**

Emperor Qin Shi Huangdi (259–210 BCE) of the Qin Dynasty ordered a wall to be built to protect his empire from invaders. This wall was extended over many centuries by different rulers. It became the Great Wall of China, the best-preserved section of which is 5,500 miles (8,850 kilometers) long.

The Great Wall of China is one of the most amazing structures on Earth.

Porcelain

Craftspeople in China have been making and selling porcelain, a strong and beautiful type of pottery, since the 600s CE. During the Ming Dynasty (1368 to 1644), different techniques for making porcelain were developed along with new **enamels**, which made the colors brighter. Natural scenes, dragons, and **legends** were all hand-painted. Today, Ming vases are very valuable.

Painting pictures

For hundreds of years, Chinese artists have painted images from nature, particularly birds, flowers, or blossoms. Many paintings have included writing, too. In 2011 a modern painting by Qi Baishi was sold for more than $65 million.

China is famous for its silk and silk painting. Using quick brushstrokes, artists use colored inks to paint words and pictures on kites, fans, and screens.

These hand-painted porcelain vases are nearly 400 years old.

Ai Weiwei (born 1957)

Ai Weiwei is a Chinese artist, photographer, and designer. His artwork has been displayed in galleries all around the world, including in New York and Los Angeles. An example of his work is his *Sunflower Seeds* installation. This was made up of 100 million porcelain seeds.

Did you know?

A Chinese legend says that Empress Leizu was the first person to discover silk more than 5,000 years ago. The story goes that she was sitting under a mulberry tree in her palace garden when a silk moth cocoon dropped into her cup of tea. As she pulled the cocoon out, it unraveled into a single thread of pure silk. After this discovery, the Chinese started to make silk and sold it across the world.

Artists use brushes to write and paint on silk.

Writing and literature

Writing and paper are central to Chinese culture. Paper was invented in China about 105 CE, during the Han Dynasty. Bamboo stems or wood from the paper mulberry tree were soaked and boiled with lime. The pulp was then pressed flat and dried to make paper. Pi Sheng invented a printing press in the early 1000s CE, and books started to be printed.

What is calligraphy?

Calligraphy is beautiful, decorative handwriting. The Chinese word for it is *shufa*, and it is considered a great art. Children as young as five can go to calligraphy classes on the weekends. In 2009 an 1000s CE scroll by Huang Tingjian was sold for over $67 million.

Did you know?

Chinese writing is made up of over 47,000 different characters, but some of these are rarely used. Most people use 3,000 to 4,000 in their daily lives.

Calligraphers practice for many years to perfect the art of writing with a brush.

Books and ideas

At various times in history, books have been banned in China, when the rulers believed the ideas in them were anti-government and dangerous. Today, there is greater freedom of reading, but there is still some **censorship**.

Wang Xizhi (303–361 CE)

Wang Xizhi was a calligrapher, and he is still regarded as the finest ever. Emperor Taizong admired his works so much that he is supposed to have some of Wang's work buried with him.

Clothes and fashion

Today, lots of Chinese people wear clothes from the United States and Europe, such as jeans and suits. In the countryside, handmade cotton tunic suits, known as Mao suits, are still worn. This style of suit was introduced around 1950 as a form of national dress. (See page 28 for more information on regional clothes.)

In ancient China, emperors and **officials** wore long silk **embroidered** gowns called dragon robes. Court officials also wore badges to show their rank. For special occasions today, women might wear a dark robe called a *xuanduan*, and men might wear a silk-embroidered *tangzhuang* jacket.

The silk cheongsam or *qipao* dress is still popular today.

Ma Ke (born 1971)

Ma Ke is a Chinese fashion designer with her own fashion house called Wu Yong. She has shown her designs at shows around the world. She is inspired by traditional Chinese weaving and design. She also thinks it is important to protect the environment, so she uses recycled materials in her clothes.

Jewelry

Chinese artists have been making silver, gold, and **jade** jewelry for over 4,000 years. In ancient China, men and women wore jewelry to show their **nobility** and wealth. Jewelry was put in the graves of important people. Then and now, the designs are influenced by **Buddhist symbols**. Jade was used for rings, headdresses, earrings, and combs.

This jade comb dates from the 800s BCE.

CUSTOMS, ACTIVITIES, AND COMMUNISM

Chinese people take part in many sports and activities that are good for physical strength as well as mental and spiritual health. Some sports invented in China have spread overseas and are now practiced by millions of people worldwide.

Martial arts

Martial arts are an ancient system of fighting, self-defense, and honor. Many Asian countries have their own styles of martial art, and these are sometimes linked to religions, such as Buddhism. *Wushu* means "military skill" and is the general word for Chinese martial arts, such as *taijiquan* (shadow boxing). Historically, Chinese martial arts schools were secretive. This was to ensure national security and not give any information to China's enemies.

YOUNG PEOPLE

There are many martial arts schools in northern China. Because martial arts are a way of life as well as a form of self-defense, these schools are often based in temples and are run by monks. Students take classes in **philosophy**, health, and **meditation** as well as martial arts.

Fighting with honor

Martial arts students are taught a code
of ethics (a sense of right and wrong).
It means acting honorably and respecting their opponents.
To practice, students fight each other. They also practice
qigong, which is a way of breathing in time with your
movements, for maximum control.

Jet Li (born 1963)

Jet Li is a Chinese actor and former champion martial
artist. He has made many martial arts and action
movies in both China and the United States, including
Shaolin Temple (1982), *Once Upon A Time in China*
(1991), *Hero* (2002), and *The Expendables* (2010).

Sports and games

Chinese people enjoy a mixture of traditional and modern games and activities. Board games such as chess, *majiang* (also known as *mahjong*), and *weiqi* were invented in China. *Weiqi* is believed to be over 2,000 years old. Two players use white and black stones to gain territory on a grid. In public parks throughout China, people meet to play these games. *Weiqi* and *majiang* are now played all over the world.

Chinese people today enjoy Western sports such as horse racing, skateboarding, golf, and swimming. At the 2008 Olympic Games in Beijing, Chinese athletes won 100 medals. In 2011 Li Na became the first Chinese tennis player to win a **Grand Slam** when she won the French Open tournament.

In *majiang* four players use 144 tiles with different Chinese characters and symbols on them.

Yao Ming (born 1980)

Yao Ming is 7 feet, 6 inches (2.29 meters) tall! Before he retired, Yao played basketball for the Houston Rockets in the NBA. He was the highest-paid Chinese athlete in the world.

Dancing and dragon boats

Many older people in China enjoy ballroom dancing classes. These often take place in parks. Younger people prefer dragon boat racing, which involves paddling to a drumbeat. Every year since 1976, an international dragon boat competition has been held in Hong Kong harbor.

Dragon boats have been raced in China for over 2,000 years.

Politics and culture

China's government is made up of just one party, the Chinese **Communist** Party. The party has very strong ideas about how the country should be organized and how people should live. This has had a dramatic effect on Chinese culture.

Mao Zedong (1893–1976) was the first communist leader of China. He ruled from 1949 until his death. Some of his ideas helped to transform China into the superpower it is today. However, this was at the expense of human rights. Anyone who disagreed with his ideas was imprisoned or killed. Mao's ideas to improve the farming industry resulted in millions starving.

One of Mao's most disastrous ideas was the Cultural Revolution. From 1966 to 1976, Mao tried to reshape Chinese culture by forcing people to think as he wanted them to. Some ancient temples and **monasteries** were destroyed. Many books were burned and banned. Writers, artists, and musicians were killed or sent away for thinking differently from Mao.

This is Mao Zedong, shown in 1966.

New beginnings

Since the end of the Cultural Revolution in the late 1970s, traditional Chinese culture has started to thrive again. Today, Chinese artists receive government support for their work, and Chinese people enjoy greater cultural freedom to express their thoughts and beliefs.

Did you know?

Mao was a philosopher and poet, as well as the leader of his country. In 1966 *The Little Red Book*, a collection of his thoughts and speeches, was published. People were expected to read this book and follow his teachings. This picture from 1971 shows young people reciting passages from the *The Little Red Book*.

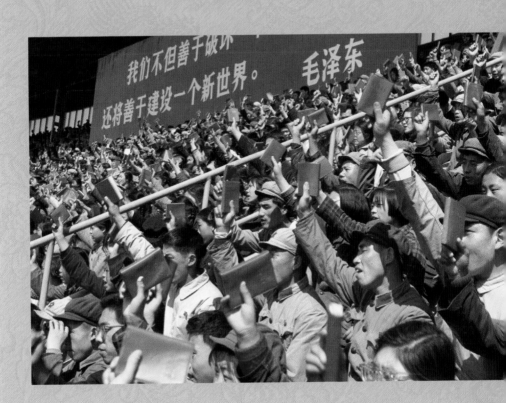

BELIEFS AND FESTIVALS

Officially, there is no religion in China. However, **Daoism**, Buddhism, **Confucianism**, Islam, and Christianity are widely followed. Daoism was founded around 600 BCE by Laozi. *Dao* means "the way," and, like Buddhism, it teaches people how to live in harmony with nature and other people.

This Daoist temple in Beijing is decorated with special knots that are believed to be lucky.

Buddhism

Around 200 CE, near the end of the Han Dynasty, Chinese people began to be influenced by a new religion from India called Buddhism. Buddhists believe that they can achieve a state of spiritual happiness known as nirvana through meditation.

Chinese Buddhist temples have towers in them called pagodas. Pagodas are used to store sacred objects, religious books, and treasures. Many pagodas have curved roofs and have Buddhist imagery and symbols carved into them.

Yin and yang

Chinese philosophy states that all living things are a mixture of *yin* and *yang*. *Yin* and *yang* are opposites, but they rely on each other and are interconnected. Chinese people believe this creates balance and harmony.

Yin (the black section in the symbol on the right) represents Earth, femaleness, darkness, and passivity. *Yang* (the white section in the symbol) represents heaven, maleness, lightness, and activity.

Rituals and signs

Since ancient times, Chinese people have been influenced by religion and superstition. For example, the Chinese believe that a house should never be cleaned on New Year's Day, for fear that all the new good fortune will be swept away. It is also considered a lucky sign to see red-colored birds on January 1.

In Chinese culture, the luckiest number is 8. It sounds like the Chinese word for "fortune." The number 4 is unlucky, because it sounds like the word for "death." Some high-rise buildings do not have a named fourth floor for this reason.

In temples, people consult bamboo sticks called *qian* for advice about problems in their lives.

Animal calendar

A calendar of 12 animal signs was a way of naming the years in ancient China, and it is still used today. For example, babies born in 2012 are born in the Year of the Dragon. See which animal represents you in the chart on the next page.

Year of the Dragon	2000/2012
Year of the Snake	2001/2013
Year of the Horse	2002/2014
Year of the Goat	2003/2015
Year of the Monkey	2004/2016
Year of the Rooster	2005/2017
Year of the Dog	2006/2018
Year of the Pig	2007/2019
Year of the Rat	2008/2020
Year of the Ox	2009/2021
Year of the Tiger	2010/2022
Year of the Rabbit	2011/2023

Funeral customs

When people die, family members burn special paper houses and money for the dead. In ancient times, people celebrated their ancestors with picnics, music, and kite flying.

Emperor Qin Shi Huangdi (259–210 BCE)

Emperor Qin Shi Huangdi wanted protection in the afterlife. A life-sized pottery army was buried with him. His tomb has not been opened yet, but legend says that it is booby-trapped with armed crossbows and a river of poisonous mercury.

Holidays and festivals

Chinese people celebrate many different festivals all across the country. The most important national ones are Chinese New Year in January or February; International Labor Day, which is the first week of May; and National Day, which is celebrated during the first week of October.

YOUNG PEOPLE

On New Year's Day, relatives put money or candy into envelopes called *hongbao* and put them under children's pillows. The amount of money usually ends in an even number, as Chinese people believe this will bring good luck. *Hongbao* envelopes are red, to represent good luck and ward off evil spirits.

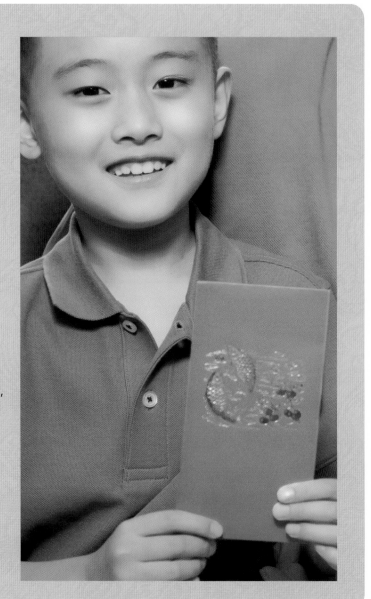

At the end of the Spring Festival, towns and cities across China celebrate *Yuanxiaojie*, the Lantern Festival. Temples, parks, businesses, and homes are decorated with colorful lanterns made of paper and glass. Dragon and lion dances are performed in the streets.

During Chinese New Year, red lanterns are hung in streets and parks.

Sky and sea

Every year in April, the skies above the city of Weifang are filled with the sight of thousands of colorful kites at its kite festival. Drums, gongs, and music accompany this international festival.

The Qintong Boat Festival has taken place since the days of the Ming Dynasty. Lake Xique is filled with boats. Dragon and lion dances are performed on the boats, and thousands of people watch the spectacle.

FAMILY AND SOCIETY

Family is central to Chinese society. In most families today, the father is still the main provider for the family. However, many women also work. Children are mostly free to choose the career they want and the partner they want. However, they still respect their elders and seek their advice.

Children typically live with their parents until marriage. Afterward, most couples live in small apartments in cities.

In the countryside, families live in wooden houses with tin or thatched roofs, and they cook over open fires. In the past, arranged marriages were common among farmers and country people. Today, there is more freedom and choice.

One-child policy

According to Chinese law, most couples are only allowed one child. This is a way to control population growth and to protect the country's **natural resources**.

In the countryside, where there is a shortage of workers, families are allowed to have more than one child. Some ethnic minority families are also given exceptions from the one-child policy. Traditionally, baby boys are favored, but this is slowly changing as there are better opportunities for women in society.

This is a typical Chinese family, with just one child.

YOUNG PEOPLE

Today, many young people are leaving their country homes and traveling to the cities for work or to improve their education. This is changing country life in China, as there are fewer people left to work the land and keep village communities going.

YOUNG PEOPLE

Traditionally, marriages within the Yi people are arranged by parents. The bride's family demands engagement gifts of land or animals. Yi brides make wedding pants for their grooms as a gift. The men then wear the pants every day until the first child is born.

Ethnic groups

There are over 50 different groups of people who make up China's huge population. Each group has its own particular way of life, language, and culture.

The Miao make up one of the largest ethnic groups in China, with around 9 million people. Miao are very skilled at making jewelry.

These Miao girls are wearing decorative silver jewelry. The girl on the right is playing a *lusheng*.

Miao have their own traditional wind instrument, a reed mouth organ known as the *lusheng*, which is played at festivals.

Around 20,000 Jino people live mainly in Yunnan province. They worship the god *Amo Yaobai*, who they believe created the sky and the land. Their most important festival is the Iron Forging Festival. During this, Jino dance to the Sun Drum and hope for a good harvest.

There are over 2.5 million Dong people living in Guizhou and Hunan provinces. They are farmers and foresters. The women are known for their spinning and embroidery. Most of their clothing is blue, black, white, and purple.

This is a Drum Tower, a traditional wooden structure built by the Dong people.

Did you know?

The Dong people of southern China think ahead. When a child is born, they plant a group of pine trees. When the child becomes an adult at 18, the trees are cut down and used to build a house for the young person.

Food and drink

People all over the world enjoy eating Chinese food, such as noodles, crispy duck, and **wontons**. In China food is cooked in woks or bamboo basket steamers, and people eat out of bowls with chopsticks. Today, Chinese people are eating more meat and wheat, like people in the West.

Ching-He Huang (born 1978)

Ching-He Huang is a Chinese television chef and best-selling author. Her cooking is influenced by traditional Chinese cooking, but with a modern twist. Her television programs for English-speaking audiences try to make Chinese food simple and to introduce unusual ingredients to the viewers.

Festival foods

Moon cakes are eaten during the mid-fall festival. These sweet pastry cakes have a salted egg yolk in the center to symbolize the full moon. On the top of the cake are the Chinese characters for "long life" or "harmony" and a picture of the moon. During the Duanwu festival of dragon boat racing, special rice dumplings called *zongzi* are eaten.

Drinking tea

In China drinking tea is not only part of people's daily lives, but it is also connected with religions such as Daoism and Buddhism. In these faiths, drinking tea is an important part of developing yourself. Traditionally, tea drinkers were important people because drinking tea showed a good level of education.

Did you know?

In the 700s CE, Lu Yu wrote a book about tea called *Chajing* ("The Classic of Tea"). In it he listed 26 items needed to make tea, including a crushing block, tea tongs, and a crushing roller.

Today, tourists visit traditional Chinese teahouses, such as this one in Shanghai. They can choose from hundreds of different teas.

Health and medicine

Chinese people's way of life and medicine are focused on well-being. Traditional Chinese medicine is known as *zhong yi*, and it is based on the *yin* and *yang* philosophy of balance and energy. It is believed that a person's *qi* (energy flow) is central to being healthy. *Qi* can be helped by eating and drinking certain foods and by practicing acupuncture. Acupuncture is the practice of putting thin needles into the skin at certain points to encourage *qi* balance.

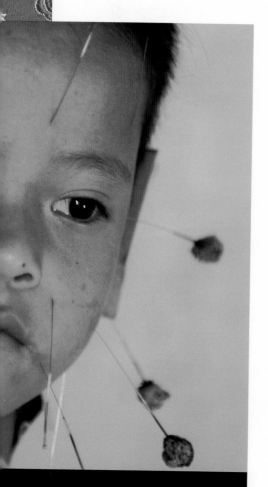

Acupuncture is now practiced all around the world.

Sun Simiao (581–682 CE)

Sun Simiao was a doctor during the Sui and Tang Dynasties. He is known as the God or King of Medicine. Two of his books, *Qianjin Yaofang* and *Qianjin Yifang*, are still read today. They include many recipes for medicines. He also wrote "Thirteen measures to keep healthy," which included rolling your eyes and shaking your head!

Did you know?

Early in the morning, in town and city parks all over China, thousands of people gather to perform *taiji* (also called *tai-chi*). *Taiji* involves gentle, controlled movements and meditation. Chinese people believe that *taiji* puts them in a positive frame of mind to start the day.

Herbal cures

Chinese medical knowledge is thousands of years old, and today this knowledge is appreciated by people all over the world. Acupuncture, herbal cures, and *Tui Na* massage are used to treat many illnesses and complaints. Modern aspirin is a chemical version of willow bark, a plant the Chinese have been using for pain relief for centuries.

PERFORMANCE

China has an ancient tradition of music and performance. Opera and dance are still very popular forms of entertainment.

Painted faces

Chinese opera stories are tales of heroes, legends, and **mythical** creatures. Acrobats, jesters, martial artists, and storytellers combine to create a colorful show. Actors paint their faces with bright colors to symbolize their character. For example, the hero usually has a red face, which means courage and support. A blue face means the character is cruel, a white face means a wicked character, and jesters have white noses.

This actress is being made up to look like a ghost. She will be performing in a Chinese opera.

Harmony through movement

Chinese dance has always been linked with religion and harmony. Many of the movements are linked to Daoism and Buddhism and are concerned with *jin* (concentration), *qi*, and *shen* (spirit). Some dances are about praying to the gods, while others are about showing fighting techniques or celebrating nature.

The Dragon Dance is part of New Year celebrations. Teams of up to 50 people carry the dragon on poles. Moving to music, the dance tells the story of the dragon and its power. The dance was invented thousands of years ago to entertain emperors.

YOUNG PEOPLE

Today, growing numbers of young people in China and in Chinese communities around the world are learning traditional dances at special workshops. These dances include the Ribbon Dance, the Silk Fan Dance, the Sword Dance, and the Long Sleeve Dance.

In Chinese culture, dragons are believed to bring good luck.

Movies and television

Most homes in China have a television. There are dozens of channels, but many television shows are made and broadcast by the government-run Chinese Central Television. News and program content are very strictly controlled by the government. Chinese soap operas, such as *A Watchdog's Tale*, are popular, but any criticism of the government is banned. Foreign television shows and movies are often censored.

This family is enjoying a soap opera on television.

Lu Chuan (born 1971)

Lu Chuan is one of China's most famous movie directors. His movies *Kekexili: Mountain Patrol* (2004) and *City of Life and Death* (2009) have won prizes at film festivals around the world. His movies are inspired by Chinese culture and history.

Making movies

Made mostly in Hong Kong, *wuxia* movies are popular throughout China and Asia. Jackie Chan is the best-known actor in these movies, which he also directs. Feng Xiaogang, Jiang Wen, and Zhang Yimou are successful Chinese movie directors who have won prizes at home and abroad. Movies such as *Hero* (2002) and *House of Flying Daggers* (2004) mix *wuxia* superheroes with stories of magical powers and love.

YOUNG PEOPLE

The Chinese government has projects and grants to support new young movie directors. Making movies and videos is very popular in China, and many young artists upload their work to the Internet with the hope of reaching an international audience.

This is an image from Zhang Yimou's movie *Hero.*

Making music

According to Chinese mythology, Ling Lun was the founder of music. It is said that he made bamboo pipes that he tuned to the sounds of birdsong. Music has long been important in Chinese culture. The Imperial Music Bureau was established during the Qin Dynasty, over 2,000 years ago, and was responsible for all official music. Today, the Central Conservatory of Music in Beijing is the top music school in the country.

Chinese people today enjoy all sorts of music, from rock to traditional **folk** songs. Artists such as Tang Dynasty, Hei Bao, and Anita Mui are popular. The government does, however, censor some lyrics if it believes they are critical of the government.

Cheng Maoyun (1900–1957)

Cheng Maoyun was a violinist and composer. In 1928 he wrote a tune called "The Three Principles of the People" for a competition. He won, and the tune became the Chinese national anthem.

Guo yue means "national music," and it includes all music played at state events. It is played on traditional Chinese instruments and is meant to encourage national pride.

Traditional instruments

There are many Chinese musical instruments, including the popular *erhu*, a type of violin. Most regions have special music schools where talented young people can study ancient or modern instruments.

YOUNG PEOPLE

The Firebird Youth Orchestra of China is based in San Francisco, California. The musicians range from 7 to 18 years old, and they play only traditional Chinese instruments such as *sheng*, *yangqin*, and *ruan*.

These musicians are playing traditional Chinese stringed instruments and drums.

CHINESE CULTURE IN THE 21ST CENTURY

Today, China is a country where old customs are increasingly giving way to modern life, but where many traditions remain. Family remains important, as do faith, art, lifestyle, and tradition.

Global impact

The spread of Chinese culture across the world is seen in many areas, from food to theater to medicine, and in Chinatowns in major global cities. Today, Chinese athletes are making an impression on the world stage, while Chinese musicians are gaining international fame. Chinese inventors have given the world fireworks, paper, and printing.

Future impact

In this century, China is likely to become the most powerful country in the world. It has the world's fastest-growing economy and a rapid rate of development in all areas of society. This will mean that more Chinese people will be able to afford to do more cultural activities and to travel.

In the last 10 years, China has hosted the Olympics, developed its art and movie industries, and started to revive its cultural traditions. It is a country that is aware of its cultural past and very firmly in control of its global future.

YOUNG PEOPLE

Through technology and the Internet, young people are learning more about other cultures around the world and other ways of doing things. The Chinese government censors online information and social networking sites, but young people are starting to demand change.

Many world cities have large Chinese communities. This colorful arch is in the Chinatown of Liverpool, England.

TIMELINE

BCE

1200	The Chinese calendar system is established
c. 1000	Martial arts are developed as a means of self-defense and for hunting
c. 600	Construction of the walls that will become the Great Wall of China begins
551	Confucius is born
6th century	Laozi is born
548	The oldest-known reference to the *weiqi* board game is made
4th century	Zou Yan establishes the theory of *yin* and *yang*
210	The Terracotta Army is created

CE

c. 105	Paper is invented
200	Buddhism comes to China
760	*The Classic of Tea* is written by Lu Yu
1000s	Bi Sheng invents the printing press
1406	Construction begins on the Forbidden City in Beijing
1500s	Chinese porcelain ("china") starts to be shipped to Europe
c. 1870	*Majiang* is invented
1893	Mao Zedong is born
1928	Cheng Maoyun composes the Chinese national anthem
1950s	The Mao suit is introduced
1966	The Cultural Revolution begins
1976	The first dragon boat festival takes place in Hong Kong harbor
1979	The one-child policy is introduced
1990s	Strict government controls over television are introduced
2008	The Olympic Games take place in Beijing
2009	An 11th-century scroll by Huang Tingjian sells for over $67 million
2011	Ai Weiwei's art is installed outside the Plaza Hotel in New York City
2011	Li Na wins the French Open tennis tournament

CULTURAL MAP

Lantern Festival

Forbidden City

N

HEILONGJIANG

JILIN

XINJIANG UYGUR

Disputed border

LIAONING

GANSU   NEI MONGOL   **Beijing**
                            HEBEI

QINGHAI   NINGXIA SHANXI   SHANDONG
                 SHAANXI
XIZANG   HENAN
           SICHUAN   ANHUI   JIANGSU

C H I N A   HUBEI
           CHONGQING   ZHEJIANG

           GUIZHOU HUNAN   JIANGXI

0   800 kilometers   FUJIAN
                    YUNNAN GUANGXI GUANGDONG   TAIWAN
0   500 miles
                              • Hong Kong

                    HAINAN

Terracotta Army

Dragon boat racing

GLOSSARY

Buddhism religion based on the teaching of Buddha

calligraphy decorative handwriting

censorship process of officially preventing people from expressing ideas and opinions

communist someone or something belonging to a political system called communism

Confucianism system of belief based on the teachings of Confucius

culture customs, social organization, and achievements of a particular nation, people, or group

Daoism religion based on simple living in harmony with nature

dynasty series of rulers from the same family

embroidery art of creating raised designs with thread

enamel paint-like coating put onto metal, glass, and ceramics

ethnic group group of people who share a common background, language, and culture

folk traditional form of music

Grand Slam in tennis, the Grand Slams are the four biggest tournaments in the world. They are the Australian Open, the French Open, the U.S. Open, and Wimbledon.

harmony balance between all elements

jade hard stone, usually green, used for ornaments and jewelry

legend old story that is passed down as history but is probably not true

meditation clearing the mind and controlling one's breathing

monastery place where monks live

mythical from stories and tales belonging to a particular people or culture

natural resource material that occurs naturally

nobility high social status

official someone in charge of a government department

philosophy system of beliefs guiding people in how to live

superstition belief that good or bad things will happen, but not based on fact

symbol sign

wonton type of dumpling

FIND OUT MORE

Books

Allan, Tony. *Ancient China* (Cultural Atlas for Young People). New York: Chelsea House, 2007.

Crean, Susan. *China* (Discover Countries). New York: PowerKids, 2012.

Guillain, Charlotte. *Chinese Culture* (China Focus). Chicago: Heinemann Library, 2008.

Hibbert, Clare. *China* (World of Food). Minneapolis: Clara House, 2010.

Noi Sui, Goh, and Bee Ling Lim. *China* (Welcome to My Country). Milwaukee: Gareth Stevens, 2005.

Websites

https://www.cia.gov/library/publications/the-world-factbook/geos/ch.html
Find up-to-the-minute facts about China on this website.

www.fyco.org/new/orchestra_sections.html
Click on the pictures of each Chinese instrument to hear the sounds it makes.

kids.nationalgeographic.com/kids/places/find/china/
Find out more about China's history, architecture, people, and culture.

DVDs

Great Wall of China (2008)

Lost in China (National Geographic, 2011)

Lost Treasures of the Ancient World: Ancient China (2006)

Places to visit

Metropolitan Museum of Art, New York City

www.metmuseum.org

See bronze and jade ornaments, paintings, prints, and more from China in this amazing museum.

If you ever get the chance to go to China, these are some places you could visit:

Forbidden City, Beijing

See how the emperors lived in the lap of luxury.

The Gardens of the Humble Administrator, Suzhou

See how *yin* and *yang* and the ancient Chinese belief in *feng shui* created this beautiful garden.

The Great Wall

Look out for incoming raiders from this amazing structure.

Terracotta Army, Xi'an

See the mighty warriors armed and waiting to defend the tomb of the first Qin emperor.

More topics to research

What topic did you like reading about most in this book? Did you find out anything that you thought was particularly interesting? Choose a topic that you liked, such as food, buildings, or religion, and try to find out more about it. You could visit one of the places mentioned above, take a look at one of the websites listed here, or visit your local library to do some research. You could also try making moon cakes, brushing up on your calligraphy, or enjoying a martial arts movie.

INDEX